POETIC CIVILITY

HEALING & RAINBOWS

Restoring Civility to Society
Using Poetry

Louisa Akaiso

POETIC CIVILITY
HEALING & RAINBOWS

Poetry, in its purest form, is less about words and more about the feelings they convey. The power of poetry is that it can manifest feelings in a person that might not have been present before. This sort of power can be utilized in attempting to change the world.

Our society and our world, no matter the region nor the time period, have always been in need of improvement. Even more, nowadays, as we all can see. There has been a decline in civility which in turn has led to a spike in cruelty and inhumanity.

Poetry has the ability to help improve that situation. Improvement can be made by connecting people to poems detailing the sort of ideas and actions civility involves. Bringing people back to the sort of values they were taught by parents and teachers when they were young is another purpose these poems possess.

Ultimately, these poems are important because of the innate power poetry has to both influence and deeply affect people. They will help spread civility and remind society of why it is important. After all, we must regain what we have lost. These poems will help begin that process.

Your civility poet,
Louisa Akaiso

TABLE OF CONTENTS

POETIC CIVILITY v
HEALING & RAINBOWS v
TABLE OF CONTENTS vii
AN OATH 1
SCRIPTURES 2
CALL ME NOT CIVILIZED 3
THE WORDS 4
THE MARK 5
THE SEEDS 6
THE CHOICE 7
OUR POWER 8
POLITE 9
KINDNESS AND CRUELTY 10
THE DIFFERENCE 11
THE LIGHT 12
THE ORIGIN 13
CIVILITY'S POWER 14
CIVILITY'S LOOK 15
HOW TO 16
DUTY AND DESIRE 17
PAST AND FUTURE 18
PRIVILEGE AND RIGHT 19
A RECIPE FOR GOOD 20
THE AGES 21

POETIC CIVILITY

LIFE AND DEATH	22
ACT RIGHT	23
OFFICIAL AWAKENING	24
MY STAND	25
AN EYE FOR AN EYE	26
EVERY MAN IS A GOD	28
THE ALTAR OF TRUTH	29
WHEN ALL IS SAID AND DONE	30
THINGS THAT HAPPEN	31
THE GREATEST RESOURCE	32
AN EUPHEMISM FOR THE DEVIL	33
FOUL WORD	34
THANK YOU AND PLEASE	35
WE ARE A COUNTRY	36
IF A MAN BE JUST	37
A CIVILIZED LEADER I WANT TO BE	38
A DAY AT WORK	39
WHAT A WONDERFUL WORLD	40
THE ONE WHO HOLDS THE WORLD AT HANDS	42
AN IMPRESSIVE EVENT	43
PAPA	45
HOW DO WE HEAL THIS LAND?	46
A PRAYER TO REMEMBER	47
WHEN RESPECT IS NOT RECIPROCAL	48
PIECES OF A FRAGMENT	49
CAN WE HAVE A CIVIL WORKPLACE	50

CIVILITY AS A FARMING SYSTEM	52
LIKE BEGETS LIKE	53
MY FEARS	54
HEALING AND RAINBOW	55

AN OATH

Standing at attention to declare an oath
I shall hold my hand to my chest, to write me
A song whose music would not leave my heart.
My eyes shall be turned right;
An inclination to the beautiful horizon
Where the sun rises.
I shall then open my mouth to fledge a full pledge:
I pledge to my fellow men:
To be faithful, loyal, and civil
To put service before self
To defend the honour that we hold
To seek first the wholeness of a man and the country in his eyes
Until we rise above hubris and debris
Until death grants me rest.

SCRIPTURES

The preacher read:
"Many are the afflictions of a gentleman
But Civility delivers him from them all
Many are the vices that come against a lady but virtue
keeps her shamefaced
The words of a wealthy man will not go unheeded
But a man of honour will always be the standard.
If there be riches and pleasures,
they will fade
If there be an uproar of many voices,
They will say in one accord
Heaven and earth shall pass away, but no single civil
act will go unrewarded."

CALL ME NOT CIVILIZED

...when anger wins over my temperament
...when I lose my essence of humanity

...when I demand values more than I give
...when I seek mine not minding the skulls I trash

...when I own a bulb and seek to put out another's candlelight.
...when I become another militant in a civil cassock.

THE WORDS

Words fall from my mouth
And launch themselves into the air.
They look so beautiful in flight,
But do so much when they land.

Those words of mine can change things
Whether I want them to or not.
I clasp a hand over my mouth.

Perhaps I do not want them taking flight.
But it's too late to call them back now.
The words wouldn't listen if I tried.
Lest the words cause damage when they land
Beasts they are and can't be contain.
Speak civilly – remember I must!

THE MARK

Tattooed into my skin
The wounds that can't be seen
I feel the pain and pull back my sleeve

Not a mark can be seen
The words people have said unto me
They stay a part of me
It doesn't matter what I do
It hurts, it pains,
I cry
I don't know why
Oh Civility, where have you gone
Come back and be a part of us
Words should not hurt more than sticks and stones
Oh Civility, come back to us.

THE SEEDS

What is a seed is to a gardener
Plant them into a sunny corner
Deep beneath the earth
Water them from an old tin can
And simply wait for them to bloom
One day soon, whether that's weeks or months
The entire garden will be bright and beautiful

Civility like seeds
We sow to others
We toil and nurture
And pray it takes root
That one day we just might
See the whole world bloom

THE CHOICE

Each day I wake and choose
To climb down from bed
And to stretch to the ceiling.

Each day I make a choice.
I choose where to go.
I choose what to do.
I choose who to be.

Some of those choices only change me,
But others, well, they can change the world.
Each day of ours is made up of actions.
Rach action of ours is made up of choices.

Each act is a choice.
I choose to be civil.
I choose to be kind.

OUR POWER

I am unable to get in the car
Without turning the radio up.
I raise my voice to sing along.

I have heard so many different voices
By the time I am finished with my drive.
Everything from songs to talk shows
And even lectures on citizenship.

A singular voice has so much power.
And many voices like on that radio?
There's so much power there that
It's like an atomic bomb went off.

We each have a voice and,
Though we sometimes forget its power,
We must remember to use it
To speak kind things and to do good.

POLITE

This world of ours has become confused.
It somehow convinced itself
That politeness is synonymous with silence.
That polite is all quiet and meek civility.

The world is only half wrong.
Polite can be small and quiet,

Barely more substantial than a whisper.
But polite can also be large and loud.
Polite can be explosive if we let it.

Polite is not the way the words are said.
Polite is the words themselves.

KINDNESS AND CRUELTY

The mouth opens - a black, stretching chasm.
The tongue works and moves,
Forming words and letting them loose.
It's the same effort from the mouth
No matter what the word may be.
A kind word, a cruel word.

It's all the same.
The effort is the same,
But the effect is so different.

The kind words heal and strengthen,
But the cruel words can only tear apart.
Words of civility take the same effort

As the words of cruelty do.
Heal and strengthen
Instead of tearing apart.

THE DIFFERENCE

My birthday comes and goes
Without fail every year.
My grandma sends a gift
Without fail every year.
Only once did I forget
To send her a thank you note.

She called the next week,
In tears, asking why
You didn't like my gift
That simply wasn't true.
I adored the gift she gave me,
But had just failed to tell her.
That moment showed me
The difference civility can make
In the lives of others around me.

THE LIGHT

Civil unrest, one reporter calls it.
Anger and hate and all our dark emotions
Shown plain as day for the world to see.
Civil unrest begets discord and tumult
But if that trend holds true,
Then civility can breed more civility.

The world may seem dark at times
Humanity all forgotten
To change the course, light we need
How to reach up and turn on the light
Civility to brighten the path.

THE ORIGIN

Civility can be a complicated word.
Is it our own choice?
Or is it in our DNA?
Kindness came from somewhere.
Goodness just doesn't appear.
If we were raised with it,
Born into it too,
Does it run in our blood then?
Some have not seen much kindness,
But are still kind.
Some have seen kindness gushing
and flowing from birth.
Yet a never kind word is never heard
Coming from their mouths.
Where does civility come from?
Do we make it?
Or does it make us?

CIVILITY'S POWER

Civility is just another of those words
That we gloss over when reading.
It's a concept we might consider,
But rarely do we think about its importance.

An act of civility can make a bad day
Feel just a little bit better.
It can be one simple act
That helps someone else
Breathe a little easier.

Civility: the easily forgotten word
That can make both large and small differences
In not just another person's life
But in the whole world as well.

CIVILITY'S LOOK

What does civility look like
When we peer out into the world?

It is a stray cat or a dog
Brought in from the cold rain.

It is a smile and a nod
Shared between two strangers
On a crowded city street.

It is stopping to compliment
That woman you've never seen before.

It is a please and a thank you
Given to a barista or cashier.

It is a small action, a small effort,
But can have large effects.

HOW TO

It is a common question
That does not seem to have
Any common answer.
How to make the world better?
How to save some lives?
How to begin to create change?

The one answer they all might share
Is that it takes people.

Change begins with people
And continues through people.

Change can even end with people too.
Humans acting with civility
Instead of with cruelty.
That sort of choice right there,
That's the answer we're looking for.

DUTY AND DESIRE

There is an ache inside me,
A longing if you will,
That starts every time
I open my blinds
Or look around outside.
And I cannot decide
If this ache of mine
Is because of duty
Or because of desire.

Is it my duty to make the world better?
Is it my desire to make the world better?
Whatever the difference is,
They both require the same choices
And the same effort given from me.
I will choose to act with civility
And make the world better, myself.

PAST AND FUTURE

There are three possibilities for all of us.
We are either born good, born bad,
Or simply born as a blank slate.

It's a shame that no one can know
Which of the three the answer is.
I choose to believe in the good,
That people are good.

Our past makes our fate, our future.
A good past makes a good future.
A past of civility will ensure
A future of civility as well.

PRIVILEGE AND RIGHT

Citizenship is a privilege, one voice cries.
While another shouts, it's a right.
We all have a right to belong somewhere.
I think that the answer
Depends on the person.

If you carry citizenship well
Like a badge upon your chest,
Then it is a right.
If you keep it in a back drawer
Full of cobwebs and dust,
Then it is a privilege.

Be a person of civility,
One a country would be proud of,
And then it is your right.

A RECIPE FOR GOOD

I am not quite sure
How to make a better world.
It sounds like a recipe.
Add a few words of kindness,
Some acts of mercy,
And a pinch of civility.

But I don't think it's that simple.

A better world is not
The end result of a recipe
Fresh from the oven
And dripping with icing.
No, it's much better than that.
A better world is an entire future
Built for coming generations
As a gift from those of the past.

THE AGES

Sitting legs crossed on the couch
When the day turns dark.
My father looks to me and says,
We're living in an age of warfare.

I think before asking him,
Has there ever been an age of peace?
He does not answer me,
But I don't think there has been.
There are no true ages of peace
Nor are there true ages of warfare.

We bring moments of both about.
Peace can be attained and warfare can be attained.
We can bring peace through our own choices.
Choices of kindness, goodness, and civility.
Peace exists in simple moments
Stolen here and there throughout lifetimes.
I choose to steal all the moments of peace I can.

LIFE AND DEATH

I turn on the news
And turn off the TV
Just as fast as I turned it on.

There's nothing good to see.
It feels like this world is dying.
I don't like to be reminded of it.
But it's important to remember.
Because if the world is dying,
Then we need to give it life.

We need to spread goodness and civility
And we need to spread life.
Sometimes nothing but a sunlit smile
Cast towards an unknown person
Can spread that goodness.

ACT RIGHT

Look people in the eye
When they talk to you,
My mother always told me.

Be sure to behave
The way I taught you.
If you act well, she said,

You'll always make me proud.
And not just that, but you will also
Make your own self proud too.

She raised me to never go without
Saying please and saying thank you,

Always do your best to act civilly.
Her lessons will always stay with me.

OFFICIAL AWAKENING

I shall sit on the edge of the window
To call out for what crawled out of a room.
I shall raise a placard for my rant until I come
To the city washed away by gullies
From the sensitive mind of human consciousness.
Here is a call to him that owns an empire;
Do not buy a heart of stone at the expense of wealth.
To the one who bosses her staff,
Learn to set right the atmosphere,
It improves your yield at the cost of nothing.
Since you raised your iron hand,
Did you not notice that ghosts now walk between
Office rooms, cubicles, and desks?
Don't you miss the relaxed calmness
Of the faces which hosted smiles in civic duty?
Wake up. Hear the
Rivulets of your aspiration,
Somewhere in the niceness between your finger snap.

MY STAND

The crown cracks deep, fissure and chasm.
On it drops dusty crumbs of communism,
and in turn, corruption drags on,
civility does not flourish
in the face of government. I run.

I compromise my stand not;
Not even at the crucibles - where it is red hot.

And like a tree, stand my fruits of mannerism
and reeds thrust hope for socialism.

AN EYE FOR AN EYE

An eye for an eye does not make the world go blind.
It rids it of evil eyes.
Every action – civil or not, they say,
Is a seed sown in the fertile belly of the earth
To be reaped somewhere else
On the stem of time.

And you, my dear, have sown
A seed of self above others.
You raised yourself to a mountaintop and
Told the people to raise you to the sky;
Such that, at the mention of your name,
A thunder shall strike, and hearts will tremble.
Well done.

Another young one watches.
Tomorrow, he shall raise himself beyond the mountain.
He shall own a branch of the galaxy.
He shall be a black hole,
Drawing harshness into himself.

He learnt it from you
- the carving out of a demigod
From aerated clay.

Louisa Akaiso

He is taking what you collected from him –
His prestigious self –
But this time, from other people.
There, an eye for an eye.
You can tell if the world goes blind,
Or it only rids evil eyes.

EVERY MAN IS A GOD

Every man is a god,
So we are told.

Everyone is his god,
So we learn.

But there are things
gods do lack;
The actions and thoughts of civility.

The invisible cord of good conscience
That minds the man-god to other gods.

THE ALTAR OF TRUTH

All hands rest on social injustice, its uncivility,
and the weighty fused hands of moment, which pause
in the dark shade, mend not the broken seat.

It lands a flawless dove
Which with one swipe rove
over a long decay of blemish,
melt away long hate, flushes down rubbish,
and lighten the dark union.
It cleanses the altar I am standing upon.

WHEN ALL IS SAID AND DONE

All the good is deed and dust.
The honour
you gave to the man
who lost his
Will be the light
The world sees.

So I say to you, my friend,
Make your deeds a civil good beyond dust
Build yourself a house
-an honour given to men
Whom the world has relegated to depletion.

You, my friend, let your light shine
In the face of the sun;
Let it light up the path of others.
All the good is deed and dust
When all is said and done.

THINGS THAT HAPPEN

Somewhere downtown,
A man oppresses another man
He says he pays his dues, so, the latter is his own;
Therefore, he can boss him through turns.
Somewhere downtown, A cop guns a civilian down.
A question of loyalty is asked in the sun-town
Is it a pledge for protection of the killing gun?
Somewhere downtown, A boy saw the oppressed man.
Somewhere downtown, A lady sees the civilian gunned down.
Somehow, by sundown, A man is formed in that boy, deep down.
A woman with gorge is formed in that girl, deep down.
Somehow, a conscience of civility would either be baked into rock
or sunk into the ground.
We all hope for a turnaround
But we forget how men mould the realities we see around
By our words and actions which abound
To be formed in those who witness them, downtown.

THE GREATEST RESOURCE

I am grateful for insights and for prospects
I am grateful for money and all it can afford.
I am grateful for ideas that propel money into
A reality before the glassy eye lens.
I am grateful for control among men – their civility and discipline.
I am grateful for machines and the oil that greases them.
I am grateful for tools that move me closer to accuracy and what we can be.
In essence, I am thankful for the gift of men.
They are the propellers of fortunes.
The tires upon which a dream walks to its wide reality.
I am grateful for men-arms that choose to be spent on this reality.
Men are mirrors that that tell to straighten a gait.
They are the flash of lightning that gives cue on dark, stormy nights.
I am grateful for the ones who are idea bearers.
I am grateful for the oily bunch that lubricates.
I am grateful for the propellers of profit.
I am grateful for the greatest resource that earth has undermined and underrated
- the gift of men.

AN EUPHEMISM FOR THE DEVIL

I know a man who
Wanted to live in the heights of the cloud;
So, he climbed the mountain beyond its peak.
I know a man who
Wanted to be the commander general,
Like the chief of the armed forces.
He thought: to be one that commands the charade of respects,
Put on the attitude whose magnet would attract accolades.
So he orchestrated himself into a requiem for greatness.
He – a goliath, looks down on men like dwarfs of Lilliput.
He – Stripped bare of dignity, and devoid of emotions and civility
To towards others –
Keeps his almightiness.
His mouth was a whip to lash.
His tongue, a tormenter to bruise.
His roar, a demon that innocent creatures out of their hidden corners.
He smiled to himself for an accomplished feat.
He was oblivious;
He had made a desolate wasteland out of himself – A euphemism for the devil.

FOUL WORD

If ever I say a foul word,
If ever my regard
I lose;
for law and country,
for man and foe;
Remind me. Of my honour.

For it is honour, to labour and to keep
to keep on, the fire
Of passion, burning in your heart
for law and country,
for man and foe.

THANK YOU AND PLEASE

To the one who says "thank you and please"
Thank you, please don't stop.
To the gentleman and lady
who will uphold the culture of civility
Dear Sir,
Lovely ma'am,
May good fortune find you.
We are half starved
for what we knew
For 'cool'
civility has been laid to rest

WE ARE A COUNTRY

We are a country, A tribe.
In my country, every city wears a face
Of knives slicing frozen, fresh fishes,
Skillfully peeled sweet oranges,
rusty trays wielding shiny goods,
gutters full of heavy smell,
colours from broken headlights,
faulty street lights, and
women and men pushing into one another.
We are a tribe of many faces
one is bloody bruised
the other is fearfully calm
one is carved into namelessness.
We are a country, A tribe.
One people with a culture that genuflects
prostrates in greeting to all others
We will say no disdainful worships
We are a country
We are one.

IF A MAN BE JUST

If a man be Just
He will esteem another higher than he.
If he be Civil
He will cast lots and be refined
He will behave himself wisely
He will cause no ill.

A CIVILIZED LEADER I WANT TO BE

I want my call to be the sweet sound of tolling bells.
I want my face to call a thousand nation
-each, reflecting where adjustment can be done.
I want to be a success, with a mighty arm of gentleness
A care for a soul, and warmth unto another,
That way, we get to bond into each other.
There is a picture in my head:
I, a success among people,
I want no distinction between how we look and relate.

A DAY AT WORK

There had been a serious shock.
The weather was cold and
We all felt the pressure that was crushing the company.
"It will all end like a lightening splint," A staff said
"If we ever survive, we would walk through the cold hands of death"
Another whispered.
The tension grew...
The CEO came with a smile
He maintained his usual calmness.
He shook hands with everyone, as always.
He said it is part of life;
To go very high, and sometimes so low.
While he was talking,
The janitor broke the screen on the wall.
She trembled.
The CEO says it is okay; it could have been anyone.
We held a toast
To good times and better days.
During a personal conversation, later that day,
He says,
no matter the tragedy,
No one deserves a treatment to stir the feel of a lesser human.

WHAT A WONDERFUL WORLD

I see a world where the trees bow in reverence to the wind;
Not because the wind is the elder.
It is a language of peace; a honour for the breezy sojourner.

I see a world where fishes course the bowels
Of the oceans with their heads bowed
Not because the sea could swallow them,
But because respect is an index –a reciprocal of two factors.

I see a child rise to call out his brother,
Begotten from a different womb.
'Let us build a house of sand and live in together', he said.
What a world of indifference;
Not minding what grade differential exists between them.

I learn from life.
I see a humble earth allowing the glory of the grass to rise on its surface
The grass is humble, allowing the perching of the dew.

Louisa Akaiso

The dew is humble, giving a sensation of coolness to the legs that walk across its lawn.

From the land to the seas,
From fishes to the heartiness of a child,
All I see is a wonderful world.

THE ONE WHO HOLDS THE WORLD AT HANDS

To you who hold the world of your world at ransom
I write this poem.

Why, on your own, do you want to own the world?
You raise a serpentine tongue;
Lashing anyone whom you would.
You raise a blow in your palm;
Slam it on your subordinate's desk.

The target is set.
The market is ripe.
We must do all we can to reach the plan
So you let fire course your vein
And pour it into the face of your colleagues.
To you who hold the world of your world at ransom,
I show this soot.

No you not that a result gotten from pressure could burn the skin?
No you not that the people brewed into your world
Would only let the let of your let be let and nothing more?
No you not that at the city of fire, nothing is in its stable state?

To you who hold the world of your world at ransom,
I write this note, to check if you know what you want or know not.

AN IMPRESSIVE EVENT

Just when I thought life was getting over,
Like the glory of the Rosemallows sleeping with the sun,
As we advance in days...
The other day, at the riverside,
I saw two people holding knives to the throat of a topic,
Dissecting it into body parts like they do cadavers in morgues.
The argument rose a crescendo into the fluid embers of volcano.
One side tears the topic with a pickaxe
The other, with a grinding disc.
We, the onlookers stood afar,
Holding their words at arm's length.
Something got us all glued to the scene
Like ants would around sugar.
They conversed intelligently.

However, while they tore the topics into bits
And pieces of uncertain statistics,
Their respect for each other held still.
None went beyond the boundary of discuss to shade the other.
None painted the other a fool

POETIC CIVILITY

For thinking his thoughtful thought from a tardy think tank.
Just when I thought life was getting over,
Like the glory of the Rosemallows, sleeping with the sun,
As we advance in days,
Some folks showed me civility is not six feet below, yet.

PAPA

I turned my father into a book
-at his stricken, grey age.

I flipped his as leaves, one page running into another
-he seemed to be a tongue of his own,
a language to be uttered at his own shrine.

No, this language is not extra-terrestrial.
-not an imported alien for a local tribe.

In every leaflet, I see the subject –a man –my father
Torn into bits of particles given to molecules that are not his.
I saw other particles of strange molecules finding home in his body.

This book tells the story of a man who does not own himself,
-this house is not for me, it says.

This poetic collection narrates the story of a one who worries to not give enough
-this house is too big for me, it says.

In this book is the language of a man's soul:
How no one is meant to be a lone ranger
In a field of uneven soldiers.

HOW DO WE HEAL THIS LAND?

How did we get here –
A spiteful state of spitting throes?

The government complains of a people
without consideration for others.
The leader says his subordinates lacks the
workmanship spirit.
He spits sourly secreted spits like lethal lashes.

The parent complains of canny kids
Kids complain of parents who would mask their love.
The pointed fingers go in loops of rants
And they come back in complaints of incivility.

How then do we get the world healed
Of what everyone is guilty of?

Practice what you want.
Teach who you can.

Start from home, to the young ones,
Then to your neighbours,
And to the society,
And at the workplace.
One step a time,
We cover the earth.

A PRAYER TO REMEMBER

When the Darkness of the happenings around
seem to engulf the light on my path,
may I remember that the strength of light is its will.

When evil and disregard for humans are reported,
daily
around me,
let me remember that love is the way to live.

When frustration seduces me to belch out cusses,
let me my peace remember;
to hold still and breathe before I speak.

When on a failing path my part falls,
let me remember that it is part of life; a path
to finding the way that leads to success.

WHEN RESPECT IS NOT RECIPROCAL

The square root of a problem
Is the revelation of its genesis.

To you who commands respect by harshness,
Respect you would earn, but compensation

Will not be relative with productivity.
That is what happens when respect is not reciprocal.

To you whom men salute, "boss", "lord",
If you remember not the rules of kindness and love

You will soon be a boss of emptiness and nothingness
A non-reciprocated respect is ricocheting bullet.

When you get the deserved return and
Our collective glory you wear as a robe,

Look at the chair which you sit upon, it is able
To tear your garment into the shreds of a rag.

When respect is not reciprocal,
The root is not a perfect square of the original command.

PIECES OF A FRAGMENT

When you hold your enterprise a me-against-you
What good do you want this ferry to arrive with?

Even more, you set it a standard of
'this is about me securing the future'.

I ask, what is a future with the consideration of just a soul?
On your quest to conquest,
You murdered thank you as an inconsequential fellow
And your ditched kindness as though you are the owed,
Owing no one the same coin.

You sent qualifications to a valley of criticism
No value is attached to the different portions of a whole
You work hard to build an empire, a piece
That will probe the face of the sky.
With the virtues you have ditched and
The hand which you use to walk this empire,
You need no prophet to tell that you are building another Babel
Seeking refuge in a sun that sunk below the evening sky.

You build another fragment by unaugmented pieces.
Nonetheless, are we not all pieces of fragments?

CAN WE HAVE A CIVIL WORKPLACE

Can we have a workplace where we would to go without grudge?
Somewhere the daylight offers a delight to attend without a nudge.

Can we have a workplace where respect would be a policy?
Without boundary. Not one sided. Respect without surrogacy.
Can we have a workplace where there is a seeking to impact values?
Can we have a workstation where everyone is adorned with virtues?

Can we have a workplace that does not have another Hitler
Holding a Hiroshima bomb in his mouth, sitting at a desk, thither?
Can we have a workplace where everyone is appreciated;
And their commitment to growth, compensated?

Can we have a workstation where energy is spent with joy, rather
Than one from a pressure cooker?

Louisa Akaiso

Can we have a workplace where abuses are banished
To a lake, somewhere in Tarshish?
Can we have a workplace where equity is offered
To those on varying pedestals of commitment via services offered?

CIVILITY AS A FARMING SYSTEM

Where relationships are mounted in valuable heaps,
A weather of understanding is studied
To know the times and seasons that a man is propelled to yield
And how to manage the shortcomings of uneven growth.

Cultivating a civil culture
Builds barns of relationships beyond formality
And irrigates the land of human perspectives.

The practice is a mixed culture
Where responsibility is groomed with consideration
The end will be a harvest of non-toxic products;
improved, bettered.

LIKE BEGETS LIKE

If there is a future you would like,
Begin to build from where you are.

If there is a feature you'd love to see,
Teach it to the young ones around you.

If there's a parent you want for your kids,
Parent them in like manner, too.

If there's an atmosphere you wish,
Make plans to set it up, yourself

If there's a sunset you have imagined,
Prepare your shade to laud its view.

If there's a culture you'd want practiced,
Launch the first of its practices.

MY FEARS

How the admired have become shadows!
I am scared of a tomorrow beyond now:
Of a beauty fading in the eyes of its owner,
Of an oceanic turbulence throwing away its own water.

I am scared:
of shadows walking out on their own figures
when they have not learned the weight of light. I
wish the world knows what it does every time kindness
is nipped by its bud.

I am scared:
Of what the world will become
When suppression and oppression are dished
Because a value is categorized to be above another.

I am scared:
Of what the world will become
When a victim of oppression transfers his aggression
And the oppressed suppresses another only for the
cycle to keep moving.

I am scared of this place
How it will look like, tomorrow,
When the admired figures of human essences
Become shadows; fading from umbra into penumbra
and into nothingness.

HEALING AND RAINBOW

Healing! To those who hope for the sun to set on their frowns
And the gentle, shiny lights of the morning dawn with smiles on their faces.
I know you have endured the hurts so much
And you have longed for the soothing stems to heal
I know you have offered so much strength, leaning on
The pole that brought you disdain.
Let your tears flow...
F l o w...
O
L   W
F   W...

...W
O
L
F...

Let them wash the hurting grief
Let them spite the goodness that others ignore
Let them wash your eyes of its dirt
Let them cease, then
Breathe.
Now, see with your eyes, without dirt,

POETIC CIVILITY

Look at the rainbow on the sky of your own awesomeness
Hold on, you will soon be arrayed
In the cotton and linen of comfort you have always deserved.

www.ingramcontent.com/pod-product-compliance
Lightning Source LLC
Chambersburg PA
CBHW071414290426
44108CB00014B/1823